SONGS FOR SIGHT-SINGING

VOLUME 1

Junior High School—TB

Compiled by
Mary Henry and Marilyn Jones

Consulting Editor
Dr. Ruth Whitlock
Director of Music Education Studies
Texas Christian University

B-374

Southern
MUSIC

TABLE OF CONTENTS

B-374

PREFACE

SONGS FOR SIGHT SINGING provides a collection of literature for use in the choral classroom. Each selection was composed according to criteria designed by Texas secondary choral directors and commissioned by the Texas University Interscholastic League for use in its annual sight singing contest. These graded materials were created specifically for young musicians by recognized composers and comprise a valuable resource as they contain many of the problems encountered in sight singing. This collection can be used effectively as a supplement to the daily instructional sight singing program after an approved system (movable "do", fixed "do" or numbers) and a rhythm system are established within the choral curriculum.

TRUST
(TB)

DEANA COLLINS

C.M. SHEARER

BRAVE TEXANS

U.I.L. Sight Reading Selection for Class C

Words by LEONARD WAGGONER **Music by BOBBY L. SILTMAN**

B-374

6

T: Here in Tex - as most of all, sto - ry of the gal - lant's fall.
(Down)

B: Here in Tex - as most of all, sto - ry of the gal - lant's fall.
(Down)

T: Al - a - mo, a sa - cred shrine a - bout a day of no sun - shine.

B: Al - a - mo, a sa - cred shrine a - bout a day of no sun - shine.

T: San - ta An - na's fight - ing men, Crushed the brave men all with - in.

B: San - ta An - na's fight - ing men, Crushed the brave men all with - in.

GALLANT MEN

U.I.L. Sight Reading Selection for Class C

Words and Music by
BOBBY L. SILTMAN

Throughout the ages there have been gallant men.

Brave, noble leaders whose courage now as then.

These men of courage, their voices ring forth clear.

Hear now the message of freedom for all men.

"Give me liberty, or give me death."

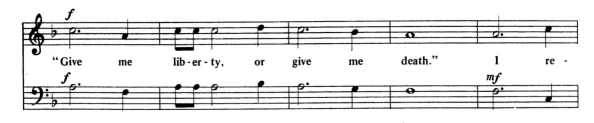

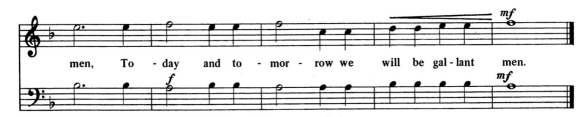

HARK, THE VESPER HYMN IS STEALING

(TB or TTB*)

THOMAS MOORE (1779-1852)

Russian Melody
Arranged by BOBBY L. SILTMAN

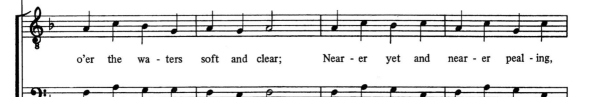

* When sung in three parts, tenor parts could interchange allowing Tenor I to sing
all higher notes, while the Tenor II sings all lower notes.

B-374

12

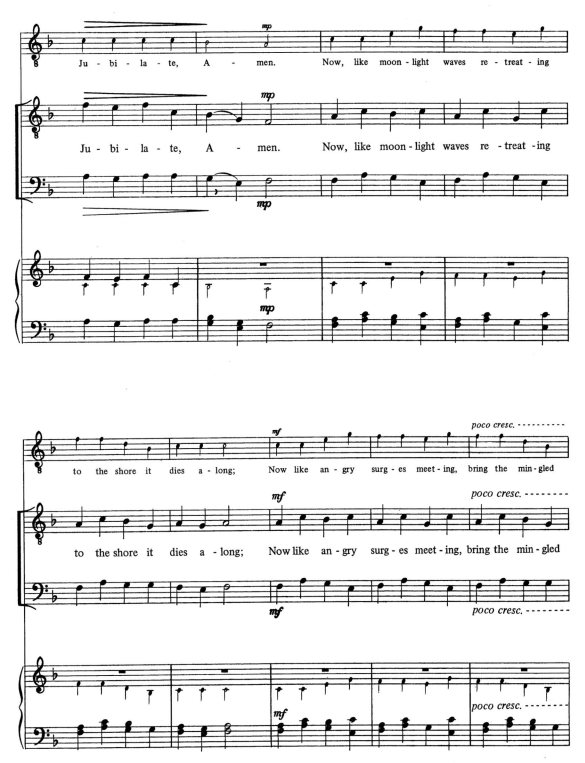

14

B-374

Men of Iwo Jima

(REVISED VERSION)

TB

U.I.L. Sight Reading Selection for Class C

LEONARD WAGGONER

BOBBY L. SILTMAN

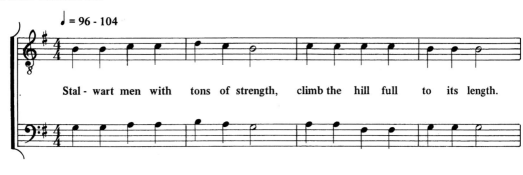

Stal - wart men with tons of strength, climb the hill full to its length.

Hearts of gold with their own flag, nev - er once did spir - its sag.

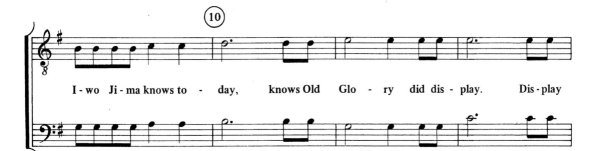

I - wo Ji - ma knows to - day, knows Old Glo - ry did dis - play. Dis - play

cour - age from the four who dared. Love for free - dom they all shared. _____

16

FREEDOM, FREEDOM

TB
U.I.L. Sight Reading Selection for Class C (TB)

**Words and Music by
BOBBY L. SILTMAN**

champ - ion of men. He gave him - self to them.

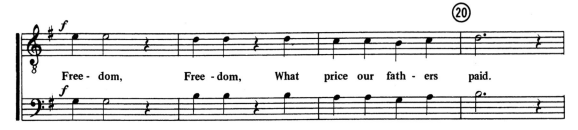

Free - dom, Free - dom, What price our fath - ers paid.

Free - dom, Free - dom, Let's give our best each day. With

Tho - mas Paine and Paul Re - vere to write and cry, "Red -

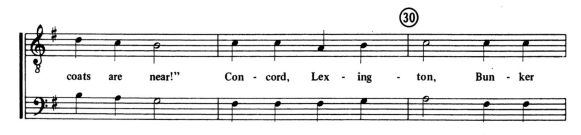

coats are near!" Con - cord, Lex - ing - ton, Bun - ker

Hill brought free - dom here. That cold dark night at

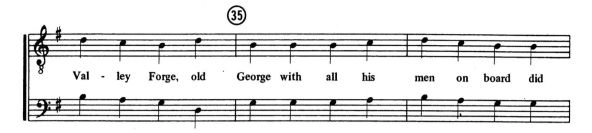

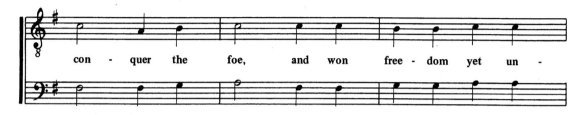

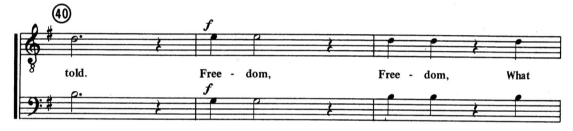

INSTRUMENTS OF THY PEACE

U.I.L. Sight Reading Selection for Class C (TB)

**Adapted from the
Prayer of St. Francis of Assisi**

B. L. SILTMAN

Let there be faith. If we des-pair, give us hope, give us hope! If there be dark-ness, Lord, give us light.

If there be sad-ness, Lord, give us joy.

Lord, make us in-stru-ments, make us in-stru-ments of Thy peace.

Lord, make us in-stru-ments, make us in-stru-ments of Thy peace.

Lord, make us in-stru-ments, In-stru-ments of Thy peace.

LADY OF LIBERTY

TTB
U.I.L. Sight Reading Selection for Class CC (TTB)

B. L. SILTMAN and
EMMA LAZARUS (1849-1887)

BOBBY L. SILTMAN

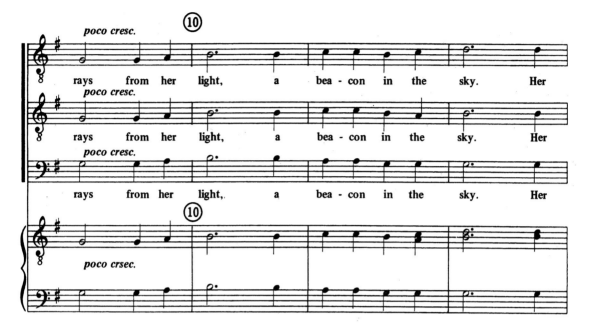

24

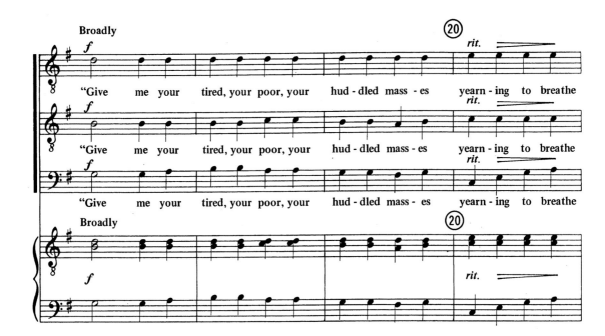

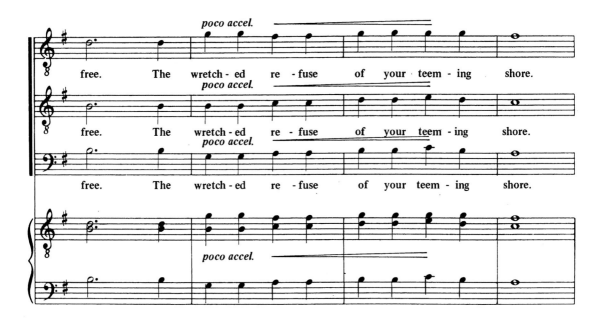

Send these, the home-less tem-pest toss'd to me,

Send these, the home-less tem-pest toss'd to me,

Send these, the home-less tem-pest toss'd to me.

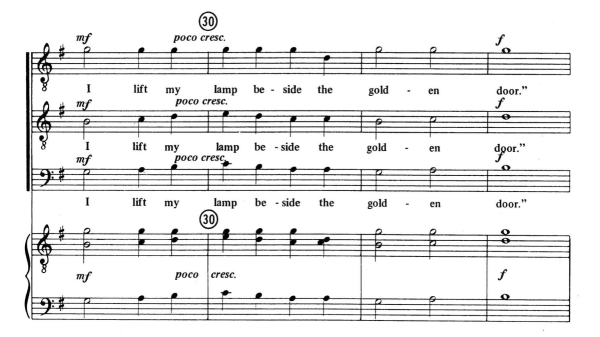

I lift my lamp be-side the gold-en door."

I lift my lamp be-side the gold-en door."

I lift my lamp be-side the gold-en door."

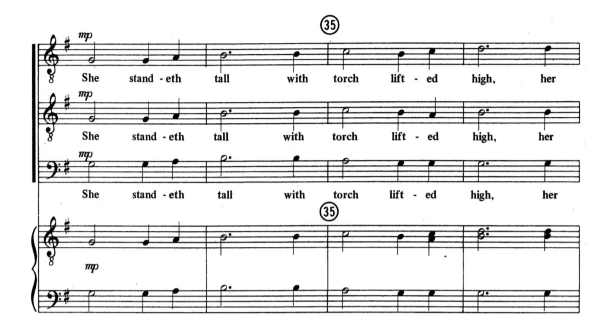

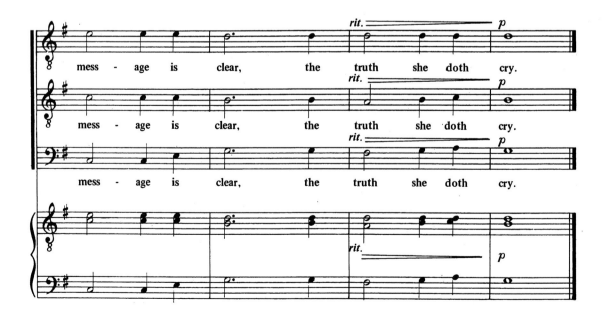

A DREAM FOR OUR NATION
(Martin Luther King)

U.I.L. Sight Reading Selection for Class CC

Words and Music by
BOBBY L. SILTMAN

B-374

dream that all men u - nite as they sing. Sing out the words, sing

dream that all men u - nite as they sing. Sing out the words, sing

"Free at Last." Join hands in a dream, the words, Let them ring.

"Free at Last." Join hands in a dream, the words, Let them ring.

Thank God al - migh - ty, we're free at last. He had a dream, its

Thank God al - migh - ty we're free at last. He had a dream, its

mes - sage true. He had a dream for the red, white and blue.

mes - sage true. He had a dream for the red, white and blue.

A BEACON, A DOOR

U.I.L. Sight Reading Selection for Class CC (TTB)

Words and Music by
B.L. SILTMAN

B-374

new.   You

new. With light lift - ed high t'ward the sky. You

new. With light lift - ed high t'ward the sky. You

stand as a bea - con, a door.

stand as a bea - con, a door. Yes at free - dom's door you are

stand as a bea - con, a door. Yes at free - dom's door you are

Your torch draws all men to it's shore.

light. Your torch draws all men to it's shore.

light. Your torch draws all men to it's shore.

mf
Stood as mil - lions have en - tered your

mf *mf*
Two hun-dred years have you stood. Stood as mil - lions have en - tered your

mf

B-374

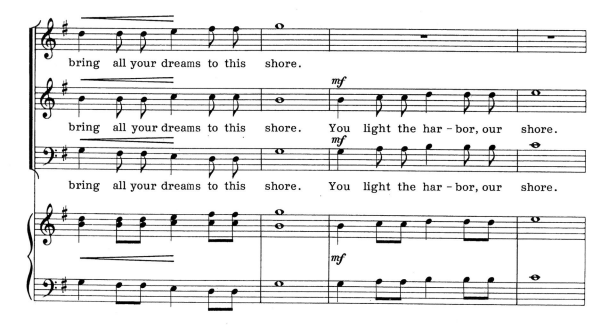

You wel-come with out-stretched hand.
You wel-come with out-stretched hand. Bring sor-row, hun-ger and pain.
You wel-come with out-stretched hand. Bring sor-row, hun-ger and pain.

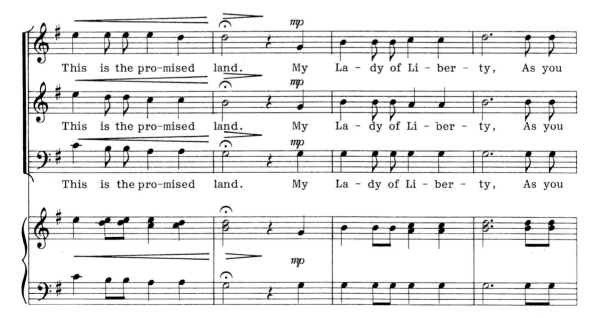

This is the pro-mised land. My La-dy of Li-ber-ty, As you
This is the pro-mised land. My La-dy of Li-ber-ty, As you
This is the pro-mised land. My La-dy of Li-ber-ty, As you

stand there be-fore me true. With light lift-ed high t'ward the sky, You

stand there be-fore me true. With light lift-ed high t'ward the sky, You

stand there be-fore me true. With light lift-ed high t'ward the sky, You

Broaden

stand as a bea-con, a door. You stand at the door.

stand as a bea-con, a door. You stand at the door.

stand as a bea-con, a door. You stand at the door.

GOLDEN SLUMBER
(TTB** or TBB**)

THOMAS DENKKLER*   C.M. SHEARER

*Text from *Pleasant Comedy*, 1603

**Only the 2nd Tenor or 1st Bass part should be sung.

B-374

WHY SO PALE AND WANE, FOND LOVER?

(TTB)

Sir John Suckling

C. M. Shearer

©Copyright 1981 by Southern Music Company, San Antonio, Texas 78292
International copyright secured. Printed in U.S.A. All rights reserved

Like the Star
TTB

JOHANN W. GOETHE

C.M. SHEARER

MARY AND MARTHA

TTB

U.I.L. Sight Reading Selection for Class CCC (TTB)

TRADITIONAL BLACK SPIRITUAL   Arranged by **BOBBY L. SILTMAN**

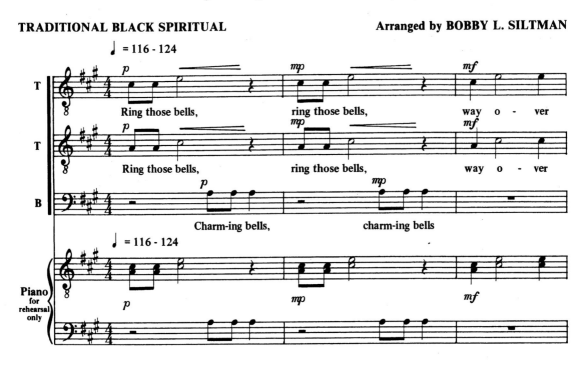

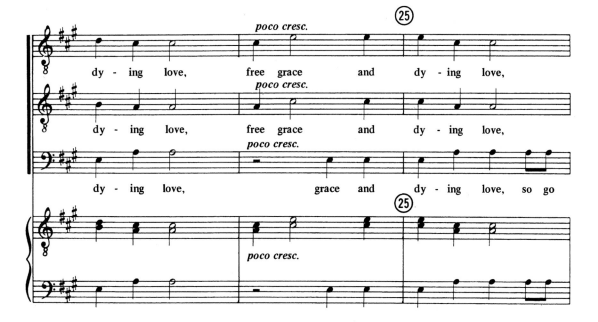

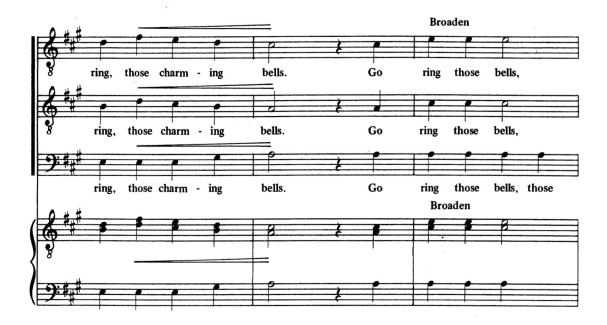

LINCOLN AT GETTYSBURG

U.I.L. Sight Reading Selection for Class CCC

Words by LEONARD WAGGONER   **Music by BOBBY L. SILTMAN**

Lib - er - ty, de - moc - ra - cy, Gov - ern - ment of the peo - ple, by the

peo - ple, for the peo - ple, shall not per - ish from the earth.

Tempo markings may be disregarded when being performed at Sight Reading Contest

B-374

48

Tall and lank - y, state - ly, too, sym - bol of red, white, and blue.

Tall and lank - y, state - ly, too, sym - bol of red, white, and blue.

mf

sym - bol of red, white, and blue.

Gal - lant man of hon -oured fame, Hon - est Abe was this man's name. He

Gal - lant man of hon -oured fame, Hon - est Abe was this man's name. He

Gal - lant man of hon -oured fame, Hon - est Abe was this man's name. He

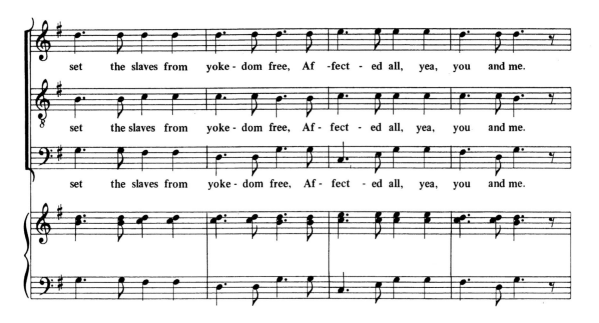

Lib - er - ty, de - moc - ra - cy, Gov - ern-ment of the peo - ple, by the

Lib - er - ty, de - moc - ra - cy, Gov - ern-ment of the peo - ple, by the

Lib - er - ty, de - moc - ra - cy, Gov - ern-ment of the peo - ple, by the

peo - ple, for the peo - ple shall not per - ish from the earth.

peo - ple, for the peo - ple shall not per - ish from the earth.

peo - ple, for the peo - ple shall not per - ish from the earth.

AMERICA, WHICH WAY ARE YOU GOING
U.I.L. Sight Reading Selection for Class CCC, A, and AA (TTB)

Words and Music by
B. L. SILTMAN

B-374

54

Oo_____ Our des-ti-na-tion un-know-ing.

wan-dered now for man-y years, Our des-ti-na-tion un-know-ing. How

wan-dered now for man-y years, Our des-ti-na-tion un-know-ing. How

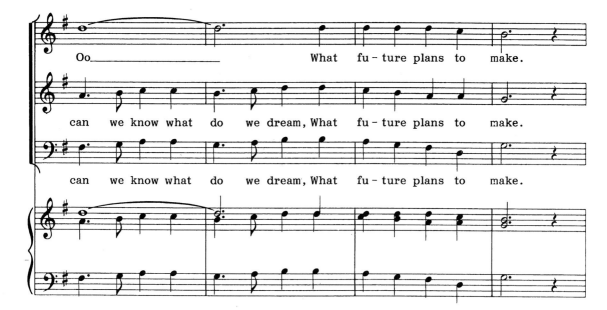

Oo_____ What fu-ture plans to make.

can we know what do we dream, What fu-ture plans to make.

can we know what do we dream, What fu-ture plans to make.

What does our land of plen - ty owe this world filled with need?

What does our land of plen - ty owe this world filled with need?

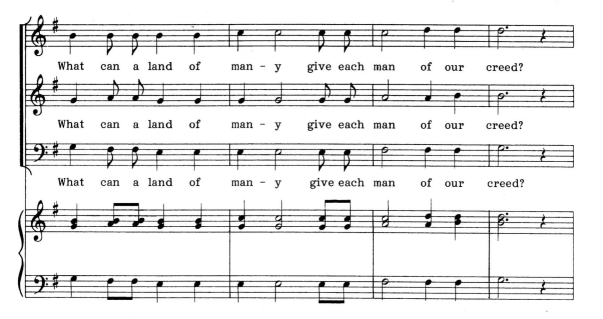

What can a land of man - y give each man of our creed?

What can a land of man - y give each man of our creed?

What can a land of man - y give each man of our creed?

How can we share love and hon - or, stamp out hate, lust and greed?

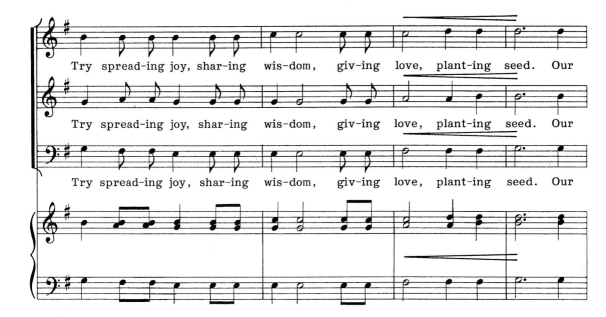

Try spread-ing joy, shar-ing wis-dom, giv-ing love, plant-ing seed. Our

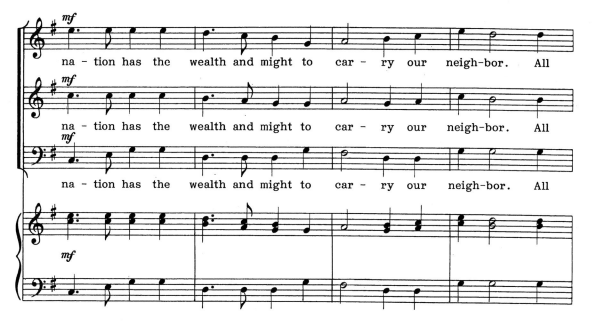

na - tion has the wealth and might to car - ry our neigh-bor. All

na - tion has the wealth and might to car - ry our neigh-bor. All

na - tion has the wealth and might to car - ry our neigh-bor. All

ci - ti-zens must see the light, give hope to our broth-er,

ci - ti-zens must see the light, give hope to our broth-er, Now

ci - ti-zens must see the light, give hope to our broth-er, Now

Oo_____ great tasks as a fa-vor.

join we all, our hands must clasp great tasks___ as a fa-vor. We

join we all, our hands must clasp great tasks___ as a fa-vor. We

Oo_____ Let's care for each oth-er. We've

know our goal our vi - sion true, Let's care___ for each oth-er. We've

know our goal our vi - sion true, Let's care___ for each oth-er. We've

wan - dered now for man - y years our des - ti - na-tion un-know-ing. We

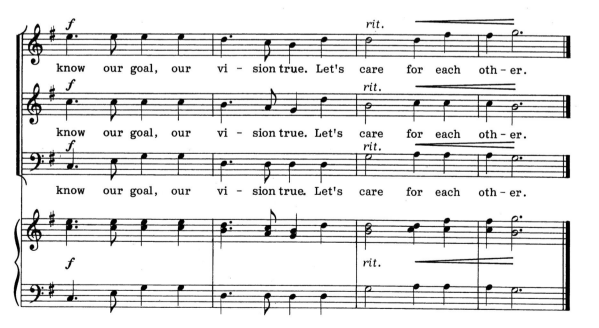

know our goal, our vi - sion true. Let's care for each oth - er.

I Would be True

TTB

HOWARD A. WALTER

U.I.L. Sight Reading Selection for Class AAA & CCC

BOBBY L. SILTMAN

Lyrics:

I would be true, for there are those who trust me.

I would be true, for there are those who trust me.

I would be pure, for there are those who care;

I would be pure, for there are those who care;

COME LIST, AND HARK!

(TBB)

THOMAS HEYWOOD

C. M. SHEARER

B-374

I. Have I Found Her?

U.I.L. Sight Reading Selection for Class A and Class AA

Francis Pilkington (?)
(16 c.)

C. M. SHEARER

B-374

III. The Man of Life Upright
TBB

THOMAS CHAMPION

C.M. SHEARER

U.I.L. Sight Reading Selection for Classes
AA-A Boys (TBB), CCC Boys (TTB) and CC Boys (TTB).

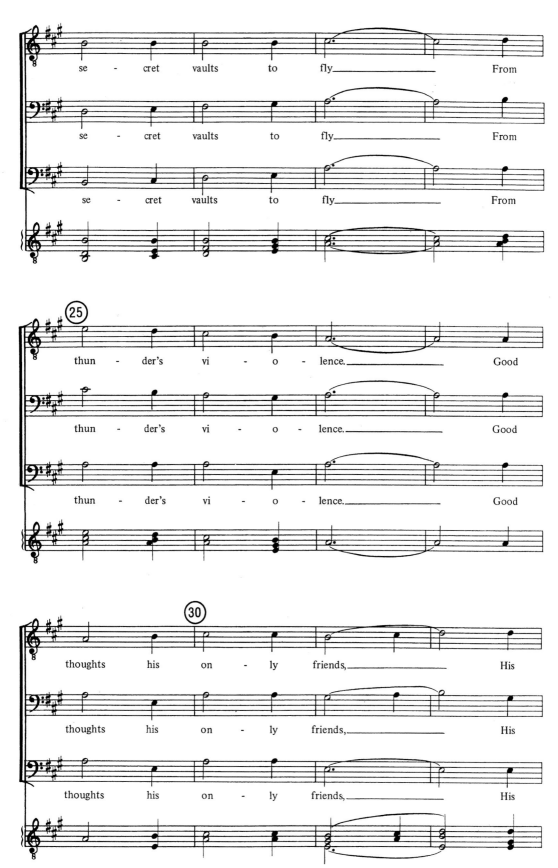